Disney
BIG HERO 6

ROBOT-TECH
ACTIVITIES

PaRragon

Bath · New York · Cologne · Melbourne · Delhi
Hong Kong · Shenzhen · Singapore · Amsterdam

Brave new heroes

Unscramble the names of all the members of Big Hero 6, then write the correct name beneath each picture.

1. BAXAMY   2. DERF   3. OG OG OGATOM
4. ROHI ADAMHA   5. HYENO MELON
6. SABAWI

A _ _ _ _ _

B _ _ _ _ _ _ _ _ _ _ _ _ _ _ _ _ _

C _ _ _ _ _ _

D _ _ _ _ _ _ _ _ _ _

E _ _ _ _ _ _

F _ _ _ _

_ _ _ _ _ _

_ _ _ _ _ _

Whenever you complete an activity, check the answer at the back of the book. If you got it right then place a **BIG 6 STICKER** here!

Big bro rocks!

Tadashi is not just Hiro's big brother... he's best friend, too. [This] picture of the [Ham]ada brothers.

3

High-tech maze

Hiro and Tadashi ride their scooter to San Fransokyo Tech to use its state-of-the-art equipment. Can you help them find their way to the robotics lab through the maze of corridors?

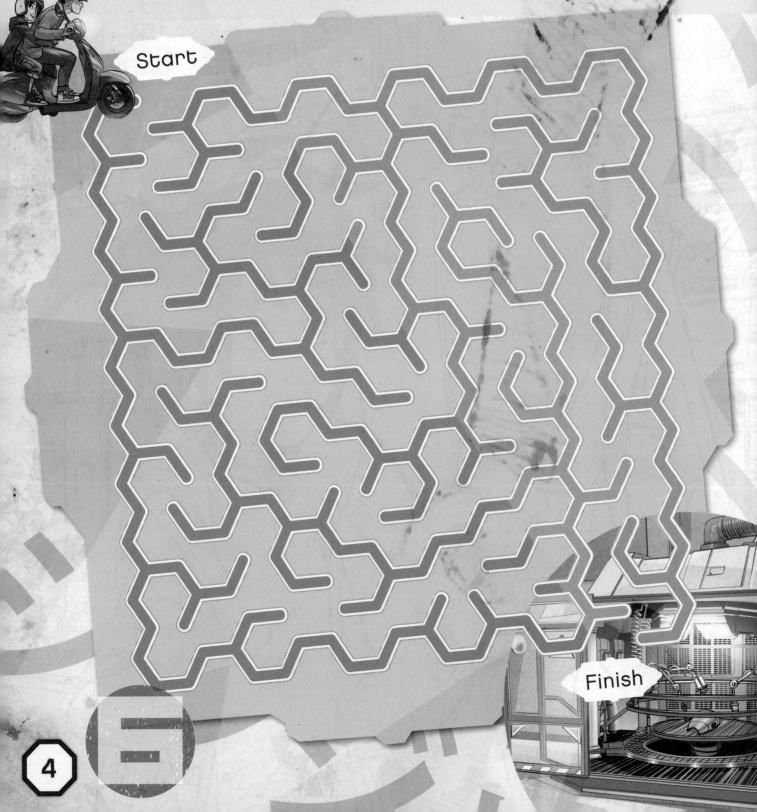

Start

Finish

Scrappy

The scrapyard is the best place for finding spare parts! There are six differences between these two pictures. Can you spot them?

Souped-up search

The first-time superheroes are still getting used to their new gadgets. Can you find each one hidden in the wordsearch?

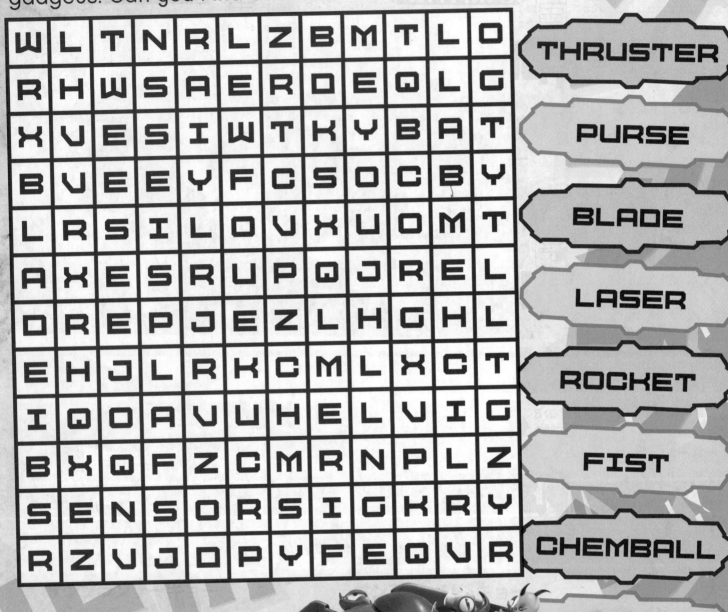

W	L	T	N	R	L	Z	B	M	T	L	O
R	H	W	S	A	E	R	D	E	Q	L	G
X	V	E	S	I	W	T	K	Y	B	A	T
B	V	E	E	Y	F	C	S	O	C	B	Y
L	R	S	I	L	O	V	X	U	O	M	T
A	X	E	S	R	U	P	Q	J	R	E	L
D	R	E	P	J	E	Z	L	H	G	H	L
E	H	J	L	R	K	C	M	L	X	C	T
I	Q	O	A	V	U	H	E	L	V	I	G
B	X	Q	F	Z	C	M	R	N	P	L	Z
S	E	N	S	O	R	S	I	G	K	R	Y
R	Z	V	J	O	P	Y	F	E	Q	V	R

THRUSTER

PURSE

BLADE

LASER

ROCKET

FIST

CHEMBALL

FIRE

SENSOR

WHEEL

Physics wizard

Wasabi's laser hands rule! But can you spot which picture is an exact copy of the large Wasabi?

A

B

C

D

E

Clone and colour

Sometimes one superhero nurse-bot just isn't enough!
Use the grid to help you draw a clone of Baymax.
Colour him in when you're finished!

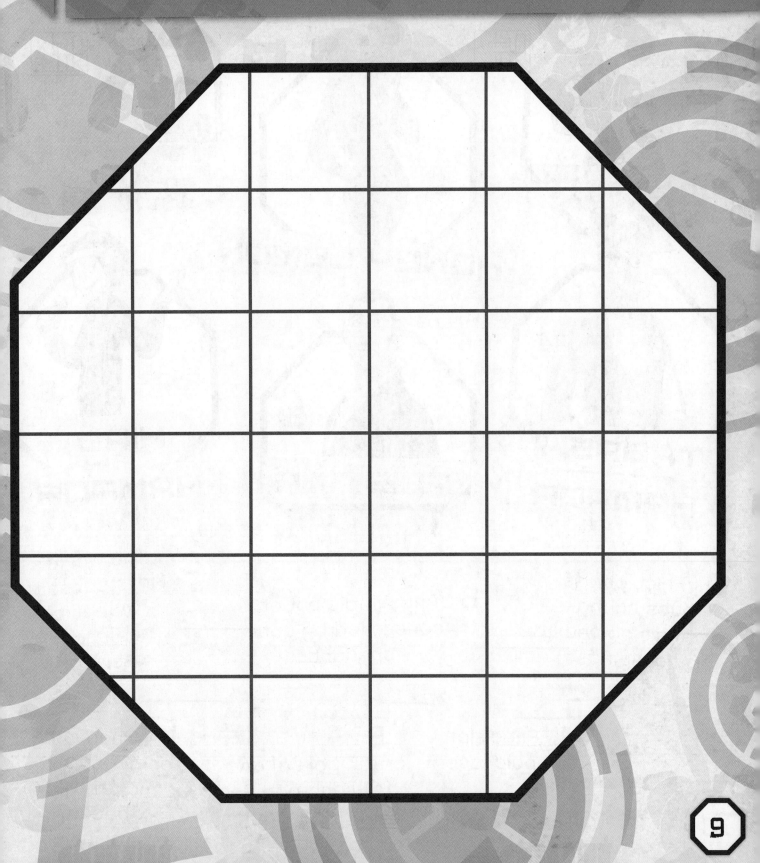

Total tech-heads

Can you guess who designed each of these groundbreaking inventions? Read the descriptions and draw a line to join each inventor with his or her creation.

1 WASABI

2

HONEY LEMON

3 GO GO TOMAGO

4 TADASHI HAMADA

5 ALISTAIR KREI

6 HIRO HAMADA

A Frictionless hubs to make wheels go really, really fast

B Tiny nimble robots controlled by your thoughts

C The world's first portable robotic healthcare assistant

D Precision optic laser

E A portal and flight pod for teleportation

F Chemical compound that makes metal become brittle

Great jets of fire

Draw in Fred's fiery breath and then colour in the whole picture. Use the image at the bottom to help you.

What's in a name?

One member of Big Hero 6 suggested a different name for the team. But what was it? Circle every third letter in the spiral to find out. The first letter has been done for you.

START HERE

The team could have been called:

F _ _ _ ' _ _ _ _ _ _ .

Boy genius

Join the dots to complete Hiro's helmet, then colour him in.

13

Junk workshop

Hiro's workshop is a real mess! Can you help him find all of the things at the bottom of the page among the tools and tech?

Can you find these eight objects in Hiro's workshop?

Escape from the warehouse

Hiro and Baymax need to escape from Yokai's warehouse ... and fast! Colour in the scene as they run away from Yokai's microbots.

15

Microbot mania

With the right direction, Hiro's microbots can do anything! Use the key to direct the microbots through this grid.

START

KEY

FINISH

UP • RIGHT ( )

DOWN ← LEFT ○

16

Inventor at work

Design your own brilliant invention for the tech showcase.
It could be a robot or maybe a machine to
help you with chores or homework.

Caught on camera

Yokai's security cameras have caught glimpses of the crime fighters. Can you work out who's who before Yokai does? Write the correct name under each picture.

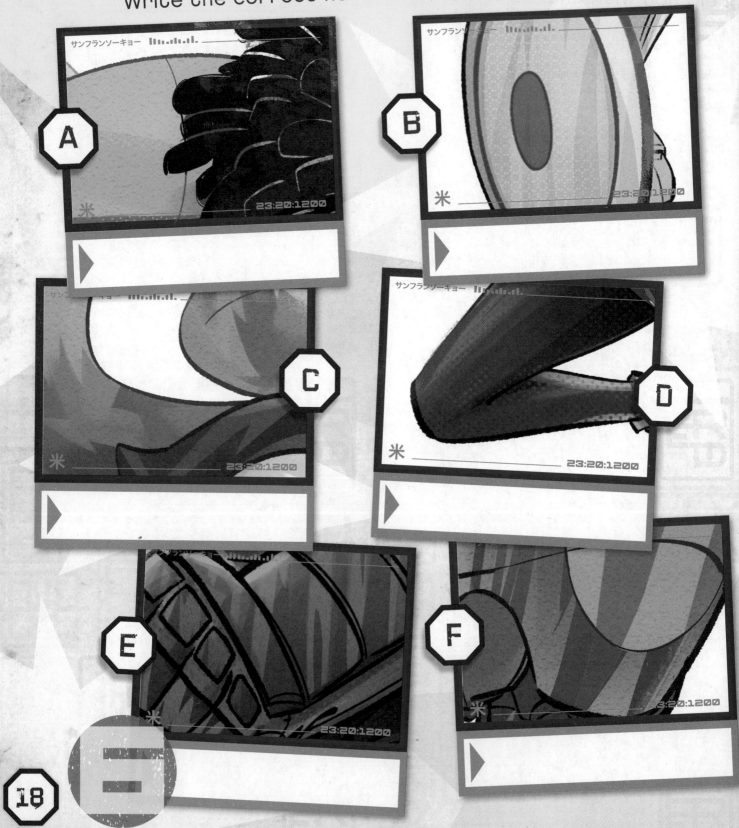

Take down Yokai!

Honey Lemon and Go Go Tomago are fighting the evil Yokai. Colour them in as they battle the bad guy – and his microbots!

Karate master

Hiro loads Baymax with super-cool kung fu moves to fight Yokai. Choose words from the word bank below to complete the names of Baymax's best moves. Some letters have been filled in for you.

1 PALM-HEEL _ _ _ _ _ K _

2 _ _ _ U _ _ HOUSE

3 _ _ _ _ _ F _ HAND

4 FIST _ _ _ _ P

5 S _ _ _ _ _ HAND

6 BACK _ _ _ _ _

KICK

BUMP

STRIKE

SWORD

KNIFE

ROUND

Portal problem

Hiro needs Baymax's help for a rescue mission! But which path leads to the big, friendly robot?

Battle armour for Baymax

Baymax is a soft, huggable personal healthcare companion ... but then Hiro creates an amazing suit of battle armour for him. Design your own armour over Baymax's original shape so that he can fight Yokai and the microbots!

Watery rescue

Baymax saves the other members of Big Hero 6 when their car crashes into the Bay. Colour in this underwater picture as they all float towards the surface.

Shadowing Honey

Stand back! Honey is about to hurl one of her powerful chem-balls! First, she needs you to find her correct shadow. Which one is it?

San Fransokyo flight

Armoured Baymax flies high above the city, with Hiro on his back. But some pieces of the picture are missing. Draw lines to show where each missing piece fits.

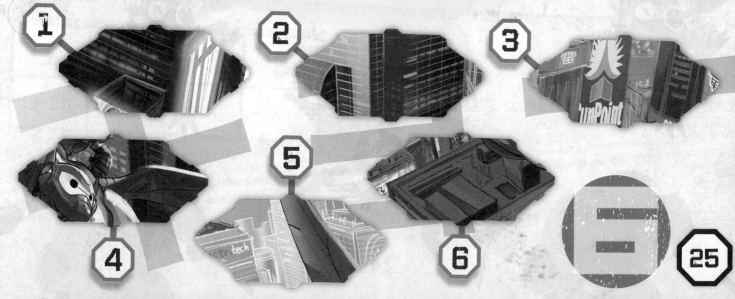

Talking in code

KEY

Where's Hiro's favourite place in the city?
Use this number code to find out!

1	2	3	4	5	6	7	8	9	10	11	12	13
H	A	W	F	J	B	M	T	R	Z	L	G	Y

14	15	16	17	18	19	20	21	22	23	24	25	26
E	P	K	S	V	O	C	I	X	U	N	Q	D

CODED MESSAGE

17	2	24

4	9	2	24	17	19	16	13	19

8	14	20	1

26

Be Wasabi

Wasabi's laser hands can slice
through anything!
Colour in this
scientific superhero!

Gone in a flash

Imagine you're a genius scientist, experimenting with teleportation. Design a flight pod to transport something from one place to another in a split second. What would you transport?

ビッグ・ヒーロ-6
ビッグ・ヒーロ-6
ビッグ・ヒーロ-6
ビッグ・ヒーロ-6
:-ロ-6
ビッグ・ヒーロ-6
ビッグ・ヒーロ-6

Quick quiz

Big Hero 6 are proud to be supernerds, but how much do *you* know about *them*? Test your superfan status by ticking 'true' or 'false' for each statement.

		True	False
1	Tadashi is Hiro's younger brother.		
2	Hiro hates hot chicken wings.		
3	Fred's suit allows him to breathe fire.		
4	Aunt Cass runs a café called *The Unlucky Cat*.		
5	Wasabi is very neat and tidy.		
6	Fred collects comic books.		
7	Big Hero 6 live in San Fransokyo.		
8	Baymax is a personal haircare companion.		
9	Fred is an inventor.		
10	Professor Callaghan works at the hospital.		

29

Speed demon!

Only two pictures of Go Go are exactly the same. Can you spot them?

Big 6 sudoku

Write the correct name in each box to complete this sudoku puzzle. Each row, column and box must contain all six members of Big Hero 6.

WASABI BAYMAX HIRO
HONEY GO GO FRED

Answers

PAGE 2
BRAVE NEW HEROES
A – 2 Fred, B – 5 Honey Lemon,
C – 1 Baymax, D – 6 Wasabi,
E – 3 Go Go Tomago,
F – 4 Hiro Hamada

PAGE 4
HIGH-TECH MAZE

PAGE 5
SCRAPPY

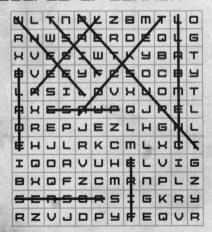

PAGE 6
SOUPED-UP SEARCH

PAGE 7
PHYSICS WIZARD
A

PAGE 10
TOTAL TECH-HEADS
1 – D, 2 – F, 3 – A, 4 – C, 5 – E 6 – B

PAGE 12
WHAT'S IN A NAME?
Fred's Angels

PAGE 14
JUNK WORKSHOP

PAGE 16
MICROBOT MANIA

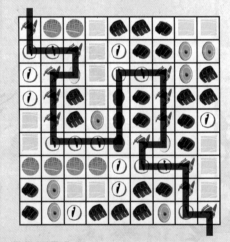

PAGE 18
CAUGHT ON CAMERA
A – Wasabi, B – Go Go,
C – Fred, D – Honey, E – Hiro,
F – Baymax

PAGE 20
KARATE MASTER
1 – Palm-heel strike,

2 – Roundhouse, 3 – Knife hand,
4 – Fist bump, 5 – Sword hand,
6 – Back kick

PAGE 21
PORTAL PROBLEM
Path C leads to Baymax

PAGE 24
SHADOWING HONEY
Shadow E

PAGE 25
SAN FRANSOKYO FLIGHT
A – 5, B – 2, C – 3, D – 4, E – 6, F –

PAGE 26
TALKING IN CODE
San Fransokyo Tech

PAGE 29
QUICK QUIZ
1 – FALSE
2 – FALSE
3 – TRUE
4 – FALSE
5 – TRUE
6 – TRUE
7 – TRUE
8 – FALSE
9 – FALSE
10 – FALSE

PAGE 30
SPEED DEMON!
D and F

PAGE 31
BIG 6 SUDOKU

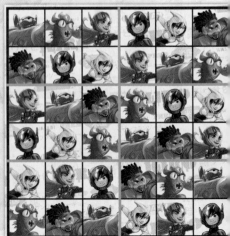

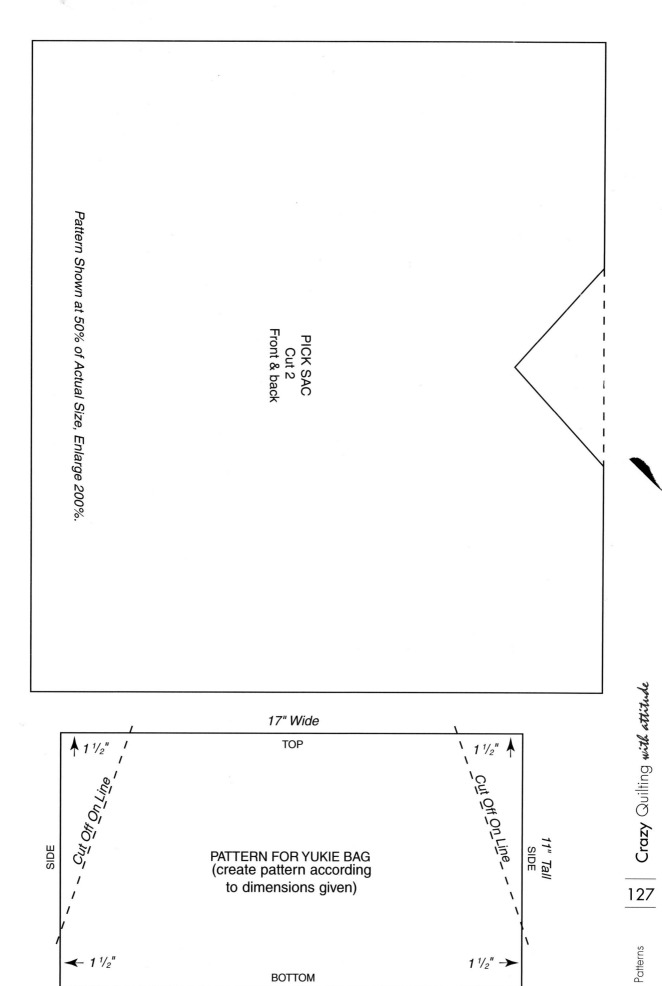

PICK SAC
Cut 2
Front & back

Pattern Shown at 50% of Actual Size, Enlarge 200%.

17" Wide

↑ 1 ½" 　　　TOP　　　 1 ½" ↑

Cut Off On Line

Cut Off On Line

SIDE

11" Tall
SIDE

PATTERN FOR YUKIE BAG
(create pattern according
to dimensions given)

← 1 ½" 　　　　　　　　　1 ½" →

BOTTOM

Index